A LIFE OF DISCIPLESHIP

BUILDING DEEPER FAITH

wesleyan
PUBLISHING HOUSE
wphstore.com

CONTENTS

For a free group leader's guide,
visit www.wphresources.com/building.

INTRODUCTION

Welcome to an exciting journey into deeper discipleship!

This book is part of the Building Deeper Faith series, offering believers at various levels a great opportunity for deeper spiritual growth. The entire series has been developed to help you grow as a disciple of Jesus Christ. By participating in this study with others (ideally in a group), you can discover and experience how God will shape your life according to his Word, especially by using spiritual disciplines such as Bible study, prayer, Scripture memorization, and journal writing.

THE GOAL: DISCIPLESHIP

Discipleship is the life-long process of spiritual development for those who commit their lives to following Jesus. It is far more about what it means to know and follow the person of Jesus Christ than merely gaining knowledge about him. So throughout this series, the strategy for making disciples will be measured in terms of how to build in relation to others—in relation to God, to his people, and to neighbors. This time-tested strategy is built upon four core biblical values, which will be developed and explored throughout this series: sharing love, shaping lives, serving, and sending.

In your life, having discovered Christ, you no doubt are finding that you want to grow in your knowledge of him. You want to shape your life according to his Word to be his disciple. As you do, you will discover a personal ministry, a way to use your spiritual gifts to serve others. Then, having been filled with compassion for others, you will be moved to go out into the world beyond your church walls, fulfilling the Great Commission by making new disciples, thus completing the cycle of discipleship.

THE PROCESS: BUILDING DEEPER FAITH

The aim of the Building Deeper Faith series is to form disciples according to the Great Commandment and the Great Commission. The construction process of such faith can be organized around five categories: (1) foundational truths, (2) life practices, (3) virtues, (4) core values, and (5) mission.

Foundational Truths

Building Deeper Faith is based on foundational truths that are key elements for life transformation. These biblical concepts encompass the scope of Christian thinking and are always at the heart of Christian love. Learning these concepts and how they help us love God and our neighbors well will help us grow in our faith.

Life Practices

All believers must move from theory to practice. That is, we must learn to apply biblical truth to life. The practices identified in Building Deeper Faith will help us see and become open to God's work in and through us, providing the evidence of the change he is making in our lives.

Virtues

Virtues are Christlike qualities that emerge in the lives of those who are alive in Christ. Virtues replace thoughts and attitudes that come all too naturally to us whenever we are living independently from God—that is, when we are living in sin. The virtues that God's Spirit creates in us (also known in Scripture as the fruit of the Spirit) reveal the developing character into which he is transforming us, and it is what God's Spirit uses to attract others to Christ.

Core Values

Biblical truth must be applied in the framework of Christ's body, the church. The core values are the guiding principles by which the church should function in love. They are our method of operating lovingly toward God and our neighbors—they describe how and why we do the things we do.

Mission

Ultimately, believers called to love are to serve. Our mission describes what it is that we do for Christ. Each biblical truth finds a practical expression in our work.

YOUR INVOLVEMENT: SPIRITUAL DISCIPLINES

Growing disciples discover something exciting and transformational in Christian worship. The worship service is the point of entry to most churches. Yet as important as worship is, believers need more in order to grow deeper in their faith. In fact, we all long for deeper relationships.

Wouldn't it be great if there were a place we could go to make friends and find answers? Wouldn't it be wonderful if we could discover a forum to open our hearts, grow in the faith, and find unconditional love?

There is such a place—your study group!

Discipleship groups provide exactly what is needed for building deeper faith. This is because discipleship goes far beyond knowledge or even worship—it can only be meaningful as God designed in the context of loving relationships.

Just as the New Testament church was built up on teaching and preaching (Acts 5:42), so today's church must be built up by Bible study. But the key is that faith is gained. Knowledge that builds faith is ideally found in fellowship with other believers. Being connected to spiritual family as we learn makes a world of difference between mere academic knowledge acquisition and authentic discipleship.

Every believer needs a protected environment in which to discover and practice his or her faith. If you want to grow and become more effective in Christ, then find and commit to a discipleship group in which you can grow in him.

Within the context of a discipleship group, there are several simple disciplines that God's Spirit often uses powerfully in the spiritual formation of his people. Consider just these few disciplines as you seek to grow deeper in your love for God through the study of this book.

Bible Reading and Study

The Building Deeper Faith series is designed to direct you to the Bible at every point in your study. Each chapter begins with a few important Scripture passages and includes several Bible references to explore. You can enhance your study by using a good Bible translation, written in today's language.

Scripture Memorization

Memorization is a simple way to gain ownership of important passages. Each of the chapters in this book includes a key verse to memorize. This too-often-ignored discipline is a powerful tool to help you gain confidence in your knowledge of Scripture and in hearing God speak to you.

Daily Prayer and Reflection

Time alone with God is perhaps the single most important spiritual practice for any disciple. Try to spend time in prayer and reflection every day.

Personal Spiritual Journal Writing

Journal writing is a way to enhance time spent in prayer and reflection. Recording observations about your life and faith will help you process what you are learning and clarify the spiritual issues in your life. Take this study as your opportunity to begin the practice of journal writing. You'll be glad you did.

May God richly bless you and draw you closer in knowledge and love for him as you study and fellowship together with his people in your pursuit of authentic discipleship by building deeper faith.

WEEK 1

SEE REALITY FROM GOD'S WORLDVIEW

———— 🔲 ————

I have been crucified with Christ and I no longer live,
but Christ lives in me. The life I now live in the body, I live by faith
in the Son of God, who loved me and gave himself for me.

—Galatians 2:20

BIBLE BASICS

- Ephesians 1:17–23

What does it mean to know God better? In what ways does that affect the way you live?

UNDERSTANDING WORLDVIEW

Christians who want to see life clearly need to think about where they stand. They need to identify the intellectual precipice that forms their viewpoint of life, shapes their thinking, and becomes the foundation on which they build their lives. They need to understand their worldview.

All human beings have a way of thinking that is the conceptual place where they stand. This vantage point from which they look at life is their worldview—the cultural and philosophical perspective that shapes their view of reality. Typically, people absorb their worldviews from the influencers around them: parents, teachers, church, friends, social and cultural environment, and entertainment. Most of us have never thought to ask, "What is my worldview?" It's just something we have. It is the platform on which we stand as we look at our world. Or, to change the metaphor, it is the lens through which we see what is around us. As people grow, change, and learn, their worldviews can be shaped, restructured, or reinforced by greater insight and understanding.

Have you encountered anyone with a view of life that radically differed from your own? What was it like?

DANGERS OF A MISGUIDED WORLDVIEW

A person's worldview has great power to shape his or her life. We respond to other people socially based on how we see life. Much misunderstanding and miscommunication happen because we have dissimilar ways of understanding reality.

The Negative Power of Worldview

For example, an African-American woman who has grown to adulthood in an environment that communicates she is inferior, inadequate, and dangerous, and has faced the constant pressure of economic insecurity, will have a fundamentally different view of reality than a

Caucasian, middle-class woman who has never known want and has always encountered her world from a position of power.

Where did you grow up? What values shaped your life? What cultural platform shaped your view of reality?

The Limiting Power of Worldview

The principle that worldview shapes and limits a person's reality is seen in some studies done by church growth researchers. Years ago the Fuller Institute of Church Growth discovered that most pastors would lead a church in growing only to the size of the congregation they themselves grew up in. In other words, the "congregational worldview" shaped by the pastors' childhood church experiences created psychological and social boundaries that kept them from expanded ministry. When they led a church to the size of their childhood congregation, internal motivators were satisfied; there was no need to push beyond. Researchers found also that a pastor's worldview defined the organizational understanding and social expectations of a congregation, so even the mechanics of leading a church were affected.

If childhood church experiences can shape the professional identity of a minister so powerfully, imagine the effect that worldview will have on the life of a child who happens to grow up in an urban ghetto.

Self-Focused Worldviews

Religious sociologists tell us that many young adults today are not motivated by loyalty to an organization, but by the satisfaction of personal needs. For example, rather than identifying with a single congregation, seeing themselves as a vital part of a church family and investing themselves in its development, some Christians may attend multiple churches in order to satisfy multiple felt needs. By rotating through a variety of congregations, they may enjoy the music of one, the children's ministry of another, the social or sports emphasis of a third, and the community of yet a fourth. This consumer mentality may help to create a worldview in their children in which instability and self-orientation dominate, rather than service, investment, and commitment.

Has your worldview affected your life negatively or positively? How so?

UNDERSTANDING YOUR WORLDVIEW

Charles Colson, known both for his role in President Nixon's Watergate scandal and as founder of Prison Fellowship, cowrote the powerful book *How Now Shall We Live?* to help modern believers develop a biblical worldview.[1] According to Colson, every worldview can be analyzed by the way it answers three basic questions:

- Where did we come from and who are we?
- What has gone wrong with the world?
- What can we do to fix it?

Whether you are aware of it or not, you have probably formed answers to those questions. How did that happen? Where did your worldview come from?

Parental Influence
Worldview begins to develop in infancy as parents pour their perspectives, values, and expectations into their children. A father's

complaint that he never has enough money, a mom's encouragement to excellence, and family stories of past triumphs or defeats are all tools to construct a worldview.

Outside Influences

Influences outside the home affect worldview also. The games children play, the books they read, and the television programs and movies they watch all contribute to forming their worldview. Many television sitcoms use the topics of sex or tension of interpersonal conflict between parents to attract viewers. This constant diet of a dysfunctional view of relationships can distort a child's expectations for marriage. There is a truism in the digital world that has application for most of life: "Garbage in, garbage out." The influences we allow into our own lives and those of our children can subtly but powerfully shape our view of reality.

Pervasive Secularism

In spite of our best efforts to control outside influences on our own thinking and that of our children, the secular culture is pervasive and powerful. Charles Colson and coauthor Nancy Pearcey tell the story of Dave Mulholland and his daughter Katy who went to Epcot in Orlando, Florida, for a father-daughter trip.[2] There, the science exhibits powerfully communicated the idea that nature is "all there is or ever was or ever will be," to paraphrase famed astronomer Carl Sagan's litany. To his surprise, Dave discovered that his teenage daughter had fully accepted the idea that science can explain all of life and that Christianity is an outdated and inadequate guide for living.

Fifty years ago the general culture still operated from a theistic bias. Because of his own faith and life example and because his daughter had confessed faith in Christ as a preteen, Dave assumed that Katy had adopted the same worldview that he held. His assumptions about her worldview were devastatingly wrong. Secular thinking pervades our culture through entertainment, the media, and education. It can exert a powerful effect on our own view of the world.

Taking Control of Your Worldview

Understanding your worldview and developing it as a Christian is hard work that takes careful thinking, lots of courage, and a willingness to open your mind to Scripture's teaching. Just as you accepted Jesus Christ as your Savior by faith, your next step is to allow the Bible to instruct you about God and his world. That requires a twofold commitment to become a learner, regardless of your age or place in life, and to accept God's Word as the ultimate authority in matters of faith and life.

What influences have shaped your worldview? Would you say that you have a Christian worldview? Why or why not?

BUILDING A BIBLICAL WORLDVIEW

Many Christians in North America are trying to understand the Christian faith based upon a secular worldview. That's like trying to find the right road with the wrong map: Their own view of the world is contrary to the very truth they seek to understand. No wonder many find Christianity confusing! The good news is that the Bible was written to inform us about God and his world, and one key function of Scripture is to help us see the world as God does.

One of the miracles of the Bible is that it speaks God's truth to every generation, in every culture. Tribal people, barely literate with limited education, coming from an animistic culture, discover God's purpose for their lives from Scripture. And sophisticated, well-educated Europeans steeped in Marxism have also recognized God's truth in Scripture and have allowed their lives to be shaped by it. Even though Anglos and Africans, Europeans and Asians, Latinos and Pacific Islanders will always view the world through their own cultural biases, in Christ we have common ground on core biblical issues.

Biblical Foundations for Worldview

From Genesis to Revelation, the Bible reveals a unique worldview. Here are a few Scriptures that illustrate the Christian worldview—the way God thinks about the world.

Genesis 1:1. "In the beginning God created the heavens and the earth." The issue is not *how* God created the world but *that* he did. The fact that God is the Creator of all that exists is the starting point for understanding the world. It informs our thinking about nature, the value of science, and even our own bodies.

Genesis 1:26–30. "God said, 'Let us make mankind in our image, in our likeness, so that they may rule over the fish in the sea and the birds in the sky, over the livestock and all the wild animals" (v. 26). The Bible distinguishes between the creation of animals and human beings, thus placing a different value on people from that of animals. Human beings were given mastery over the planet, including all other created things, with the instruction to use them wisely. This belief shapes our view of the planet and environmental issues.

John 3:16. "For God so loved the world that he gave his one and only Son, that whoever believes in him shall not perish but have eternal life." Typically, people define God based on their own experience of life. God's Word offers a wider view of reality. God loved us before we even knew he existed. He acted to save us based only on his love for us and not on any good thing we had done. God's love for us is the central thought in our view of the world—and of ourselves.

Matthew 5–7. These chapters of the Bible are known as Jesus' Sermon on the Mount. In this teaching, Jesus defined how God expects us to think and behave, in contrast with the "normal" way that most people, even religious people, live. The Christian way of understanding ourselves and our responsibility toward God and other people differs radically from that of popular culture.

Romans 1:18–32. "Although they claimed to be wise, they became fools and exchanged the glory of the immortal God for images made to look like a mortal human being" (vv. 22–23). Scripture teaches that human beings have foolishly rebelled against God and his plan for the world. Many social and religious theories suggest people are essentially good, but the Bible presents a different picture of the human condition—it is flawed by sin. The apostle Paul restated the effect of sin upon our world several times in the book of Romans (see 3:23; 6:23; 7:7–25).

Romans 6:11–12. "In the same way, count yourselves dead to sin but alive to God in Christ Jesus. Therefore do not let sin reign in your mortal body so that you obey its evil desires." Just as some people believe that human beings are essentially good, others believe that the grip of sin is so strong that we can never be freed from it. These verses help us see that through Christ's transforming power a person can be free from sin's power. We do not need to be slaves to our sinful desires. God can set us free.

Matthew 24:14. "And this gospel of the kingdom will be preached in the whole world as a testimony to all nations, and then the end will come." God sees the whole world, and we must also. A global vision is the foundation of every Christian ministry because it reflects the way God sees things and is part of his strategic plan to bring salvation to all people. Christians have a true worldview in that they have a view of life that encompasses the whole world.

What new things did you learn about God and the world from these verses?

Biblical Worldview Summarized

Our world today is highly relational and increasingly informal. We greet one another by first names regardless of age or position. The connection of the moment usually seems most important, and this often results in shallow relationships.

It seems that those same values bleed over into the way we relate to God. Our culture desires a first-name, shallow relationship with God that makes his resources available to us but does not make us available to him. The antidote to this is a deeper understanding of who God is. That is called *theology*, the study of God. A Christian worldview is rooted in theology.

There are many ways to articulate a Christian worldview, one that is based on a thorough knowledge of God. Here is an example.

- God is the beginning and end of everything. He is the Creator of all that exists. He is worthy of our worship and obedience.
- God's creation was perfect, in complete harmony with itself and with him. God created people in a distinct act and in his own image and gave human beings the ability and authority to make moral decisions and to rule over creation on his behalf.
- Adam and Eve, the first people, chose to disobey God and introduced sin into the world. The result was disharmony in the created world and separation between God and people. Their act

changed the very moral nature of human beings, making us self-centered. This rebellion alienated the human race from God and brought everyone and everything under God's judgment.

- God requires that sinful actions be brought to justice. He has declared that the "wages of sin" is death, therefore all must die. But because he loved the world, God sent his Son, Jesus, who is perfect, to die on our behalf. Through faith in Jesus, we may be accepted by God and be at peace with him.

- Human beings carry God's image in them and are morally responsible for their actions. God empowered them to make moral choices. He placed their eternal destiny in their own hands. Through Christ, God made it possible for everyone to be saved by faith. He never violates the right of people to make their own decisions.

- After Jesus Christ died for our sins, he was raised from the dead in a display of God's power, demonstrating that he completely defeated evil. This same power is released in this world by the Holy Spirit to redeem people, restore society, and return wholeness to creation. With the help of the Holy Spirit, believers are able to be free from the self-centeredness with which they were born. They are free from the guilt of past sin, free to live righteously, and able to enjoy unbroken communion with God.

- When believers open their hearts to the Holy Spirit's power and align their lives with Scripture's teaching, they have great joy and deep personal fulfillment. They will live with integrity, humility, and deep compassion for others, reflecting God's character.

- All believers should love God and their neighbors wholeheartedly. The greatest expression of God's love is that he provided salvation by sending Jesus to earth. The greatest expression of human love is to take the good news of God's redemptive love to others.

Write a brief outline of your view of the world. Is it compatible with Scripture?

THE BENEFITS OF A CHRISTIAN WORLDVIEW

We've seen that a person's worldview can be a negative or limiting factor in his or her life. In the same way, a healthy view of the world can bring great power for living. Christians enjoy a sense of peace and optimism because of the unique way in which they interpret life. Here are some benefits of a Christian worldview.

Hope

Imagine you have a younger sister, and she has been gravely ill for many years. She is a deeply committed believer, and thousands of people have been praying for her healing. But year after year, the death grip of her illness has tightened. Her suffering has become more pronounced and her pain almost unbearable. You have asked God to take her to heaven where she will be healed, and even that prayer is yet to be answered.

But because you believe God is completely loving, you trust him with your sister's life. You believe there is a greater purpose at stake that will bring meaning to her suffering. Without this perspective, it would be impossible not to be angry, bitter, and disillusioned. But you aren't. The Christian view of the world brings hope.[4]

Freedom

As Christians, we rejoice that our sins are forgiven and that the Holy Spirit has cleansed our hearts and continues his sanctifying work in practical ways each day. So when we are tempted to sin, we are reminded that we have the ability to say no. God's Spirit calls us daily to a life of freedom, discipline, and delight in doing good. Where once negative and destructive forces captured our minds, now the power of good is released in us. Our worldview gives us encouragement to follow God wholeheartedly.

Stewardship

We believe that God's redemptive work includes all of creation and that he still calls us to be good managers, or stewards, of the earth. Therefore we look for ways to improve our environment, to conserve the world's natural resources, and to support initiatives that will honor God's values for the earth. All creation groans, the apostle Paul wrote, waiting for Christ's return and the full restoration of his perfection (see Rom. 8:19). But as we wait for him, we contribute to God's glory by caring for his world.

Mission

A great impact that a Christian worldview can have is the formation of a sense of mission. This worldview can focus one's attention on the fact that nothing is of greater importance than telling others about God's love. Convinced of this, many believers choose to become missionaries. A Christian worldview forms the sense of purpose for our lives.

Jesus said to his disciples in John 20:21, "As the Father has sent me, I am sending you." If we accept a Christian worldview, we accept the fact that God has sent us.

Where is God sending you? What is your outlook on life? List some ways that a Christian worldview gives you a sense of hope and purpose.

NOTES

1. Charles Colson and Nancy Pearcey, *How Now Shall We Live?* (Carol Stream, IL: Tyndale, 1999).

2. Ibid.

ACQUIRE A TASTE FOR SPIRITUAL DISCIPLINES

———— ▤ ————

And whatever you do, whether in word or deed, do it all in the name
of the Lord Jesus, giving thanks to God the Father through him.

—Colossians 3:17

BIBLE BASICS

• Colossians 3:12–17

What changes would you need to make in your life to fully obey
the instructions in these verses?

SPIRITUAL DISCIPLINES DEFINED

Living the life Paul described in Colossians 3:12–17 doesn't happen
by accident. It requires a life transformation. Christians must make
choices that develop godly character and build spiritual discipline.

Marked by self-control—the essence of discipline—we can flourish in a positive, growing relationship with God and other believers.

Historically, Christians have found certain spiritual disciplines to be essential in cultivating the spiritual life. These disciplines are linked to the choices Christians make to enact behaviors that foster spiritual vitality and holy living. But spiritual disciplines are not an end in themselves. No spiritual practice possesses magic or inherent merit. The goal of the spiritual disciplines is not to live a regimented life but have a relationship with the living God through Jesus, his Son. Spiritual disciplines simply provide the framework within which a personal relationship with God flourishes (see Phil. 3:2–11; Col. 2:6–23).

Colossians 3:17 highlights this focus on God. We offer literally *all* of our activity to God so that all we do reflects well on the name of Jesus. That is, we choose to live immersed in the Holy Spirit. Often we must choose to live "in the name of Jesus" against our natural inclination and contrary to cultural pressure. The Holy Spirit enables us to do this by cultivating the fruit of self-control in us. This isn't something we can do on our own (see Col. 1:9–23). Yet our choices place us into the stream of God's grace that powerfully carries us along.

PRAYER

The spiritual discipline of prayer is basic to life in Christ, because prayer directly engages us with God. Prayer specifically involves talking *with* God, but it also includes listening as God talks *to us*. Without this communication and communion with God, there is no spiritual life in the first place or any development of it on the journey.

Kinds of Prayer

The book of Psalms teaches us just how rich and varied conversations with the Lord in prayer can be.

Petitions. For many people, "prayer" means asking God for help, and understandably so. Life with God in Christ can begin with asking God to forgive our sins, have mercy on us, or rescue us from a pit we have dug. Many psalms record this kind of conversation with God. Psalm 67 is a good example of routine requests and Psalms 3 and 7 illustrate desperate cries for help. The psalmists thought no topic or need lay outside of God's range of interest and power. Thus, they encouraged us to bring all our needs to God in prayer. But only asking God to meet our needs severely limits communion with him, in spite of the importance of asking.

Praise. Sometimes the psalmists praised God for his goodness to them. See Psalm 30, for example. Often prayer affirmed and renewed the psalmists' historic trust in God. They made claims about their relationships with him or about what he had done in their lives, as in Psalm 31. At other times the psalmists' prayers were primarily praise or thanksgiving and reflection on God's character or on the amazing things he had done in history. Think of Psalm 8: "Lord, how majestic is your name in all the earth! . . . When I consider your heavens, the work of your fingers . . . what is mankind that you are mindful of them" (vv. 1, 3–4; see also Ps. 9; 90).

Reflection. Many prayers in the Psalms mull over a specific topic in God's presence. Of course, we aren't informing God, but we gain clarity or conviction by talking with our Maker and Redeemer about the issues that concern us. Psalm 139 is a premier example of this reflective prayer. In that Scripture, the pondering finally led to petition.

Questions. A number of powerful prayers in Psalms ask God questions about topics on which he sometimes seems silent. Why? How long? When? These questions usually concern God's response to human need, especially suffering. See how the psalmists poured out their hearts to God in Psalm 10; 74; and 89:38–52. People can only venture to have this kind of conversation with a God who is big enough and trustworthy enough to take it.

Confession. Some of the best-known psalms are prayers of confession. The psalmists bared their souls before God, admitting what they had done and pondering the causes and consequences of their sins. These confessions, like Psalm 51, often cried out not only for forgiveness, but also for the full range of restoration in the Spirit. It is important to remember that confession of sin is appropriate for all believers.

Mixed Modes. Many prayers in Psalms mixed several of these conversational modes together according to the situation at hand. Psalm 71 is an example of prayers that blended petition, praise, testimony, questions, reflection, and more into a single prayer. These mixed prayers probably reflect most accurately the sort of variegated conversation we will have with God.

The breadth of our prayer interests provides one measure of our spiritual maturity. Research has shown that most people pray, Christian and non-Christian alike. And they pray generally for the same things: help with family, finances, job concerns, protection, and the like. People growing in Christ will learn to branch out beyond this standard want list. Our orientation in prayer should shift from our own needs to God's praise, his kingdom, and the accomplishment of his will on earth.

The Goal of Prayer

A personal relationship with God in Christ amounts to knowing God in the person of Jesus Christ. Knowing God is different from knowing *about* God. Knowing God inevitably entails knowing about God, but the reverse is not necessarily the case. Two powerful statements in the New Testament underscore this priority. Jesus said of the Father, "Now this is eternal life: that they *know you*, the only true God, and Jesus Christ, whom you have sent" (John 17:3, emphasis added). Paul cited his own unending spiritual quest when he said, "I want to *know Christ*—yes, to know the power of his resurrection and participation in his sufferings, becoming like him" (Phil. 3:10, emphasis added).

In some ways, we get to know God in the same manner we get to know any other person. When viewed like this, it's easy to see that an occasional prayer about the miscellaneous needs of life will not help us much in our quest to know God. Knowing God in Jesus requires ongoing, regular communication, just like knowing another human being requires it. We can also learn more about God by reading about him and asking others about him. That is why, in the process of learning about God, we study Scripture and discuss our spiritual journey with others. But these good activities won't actually translate into *knowing* God himself unless we also talk to him in prayer.

Habits of Prayer

Since the only way we can truly know God is by spending consistent time in his presence, the spiritual discipline of prayer helps us build this habit into our lifestyle. Fruitful habits of prayer have several characteristics.

Long-Term. We begin a lifelong conversation with God, committing to be together from now on, praying daily and throughout every day. This is not just a New Year's resolution or something we try on for size. The format of our discipline of prayer may vary with the ebb and flow of life and health, but prayer will be there year after year in some fashion.

Scheduled. We need regularly scheduled times for tending to our spiritual life: time for prayer, meditation, confession, service, study, and other spiritual disciplines. Usually a daily schedule proves to be most practical and life changing. Some people prefer scheduling time every other day because of work or family obligations. Others have more success at protecting one evening or morning a week for a more extended time of prayer, study, and meditation. It is not for others to dictate this schedule. But if our definition of *regular* turns out to be once a month or once every three months, it ceases to be much of a discipline.

Recorded. A spiritual life journal or notebook can help us keep track of our prayer life—requests, answers, topics of concern, and things learned. We refer to this practice as journal writing. Communication with God involves letting him speak to us and cultivating the habit of listening to him. This journal becomes our record of our ongoing conversation with God.

Confirmed. God speaks most clearly to us in Scripture as we read over the shoulder of people to whom God spoke long ago. God also speaks to us through Christian counsel, that is, through consultation and conversation with other disciples of Jesus (and sometimes with nonbelievers). God also speaks through music, art, and creation.

Which type of prayer have you used the most? Why?

MEDITATION

Prayer leads us into a second spiritual discipline: meditation. Meditation is carefully and reflectively thinking about a given matter and pondering or musing over it at some length. Meditation is not daydreaming. Nor is it a simple stream of consciousness. Like the other disciplines, this one rings better as a verb, to meditate, because it involves the choice to do something—to think, to "love the Lord . . . with all your *mind*" (Mark 12:30, emphasis added).

Meditating is the mechanism by which important matters are processed and brought into our lives. People with no time for careful thought are seldom able to integrate into their lives what they have heard preached or taught in church or what they have read in the Bible. They may have a lot of information, but are less likely to know what that information actually means or implies.

When to meditate is as flexible as when to pray. One can meditate while doing other tasks—washing dishes, driving a car, jogging, weeding the garden, and other activities where one's mind can be free to work on other questions. But meditation should be one of those behaviors included in the scheduled time we make for communion with God. Thinking substantially about a matter generally requires some privacy, relative quiet, and freedom from major distractions.

Our meditation will emerge from and feed into other spiritual disciplines and into our life in general. Meditating assumes there is a topic for reflection. These topics may come from the news, readings, discussions or conversations, experiences, and much more.

Most productive meditation includes two elements: asking thought-provoking questions and listening receptively for God's response.

Questions for Meditation

Simple questions are our best tools in clear thinking as well as in study. When we are reading or contemplating a specific issue, we might ask the following: What does this word or expression mean — as a dictionary definition and in a fuller sense? What is involved in this issue? What are its main parts? Why is this as it is? How does this work? If this is true, what must also be true, if we think consistently? What does this already assume? What follows from this? What does this imply?

We don't need to fear any question that helps us understand our faith better or how to live more obediently. God has heard them all by this time. And don't make the mistake of thinking meditation is somehow only for the intellectuals in the church or the naturally quiet and contemplative people. These questions can be used by all of us to focus our thinking.

Here are some examples of themes for meditation:

- How can I best demonstrate my loyalty to Christ in my relationship with _____ to whom I seem increasingly committed?
- God, what do you want to teach me through the little one that is growing inside me and will soon be born?
- The pastor said *holiness* means "belonging completely to Jesus." How would that ripple through my life?

We can ponder teachings also, like those Paul gave to the church in Colossae in Colossians 3:12–17:

- What is the peace of Christ?
- If the peace of Christ ruled in our fellowship, what would be the clues that it was so?

- What does the fact that these people are all members of one body have to do with this ruling of the peace of Christ?
- Why did Paul refer to the people he wrote to as "chosen people, holy and dearly loved" (v. 12) when they obviously had spiritual ground to take?
- What would increased "compassion, kindness, humility, gentleness and patience" (v. 12) look like in my life?
- If I forgive _____, what changes will that bring to our neighborhood?
- Why did Paul claim that love binds all other virtues together?
- Paul said, "Whatever you do, whether in word or deed, do it all in the name of the Lord Jesus" (v. 17). What do I tend to say or do that doesn't reflect well on the name of Jesus?

The Response to Meditation

Meditation is not only about answering questions or solving problems. Obviously answers come and problems are solved, but meditation is more about considering and pondering these items in the presence of God and letting solutions emerge, suggestions arise, or possibilities percolate. Meditation sends us to other resources for study, to other people for consultation, and to our knees for surrender and commitment.

Meditation is not primarily about listening to God, as we have already seen. Indeed, it is broader than that. But prayer and meditation surely are two media for listening to God. In prayer and meditation, we listen to God *implicitly*. That is, while we are actually about the business of praying for various matters and meditating on questions, we may discover God speaking to us. We hear his voice implicitly in the very process of prayer and meditation.

At other times we will listen to God *intentionally*. We have prayed; we have meditated. Now we sit silently, open to the voice of God. We are not hurried. We have no particular expectations. We wait for the voice of God in our hearts.

We should not claim that what God has said to us he necessarily applies to everyone. And we should not rush to the conclusion that God has spoken a given word to us. The church can help us evaluate what we think we have heard using Scripture, reason, experience, and tradition (such as, the collected wisdom of the historic and contemporary church). Nevertheless, God's people have discovered that as they listen for God's voice, he will speak to them over time. Meditation can provide a fertile place for listening to God.

Think of a Bible verse that has puzzled or troubled you. What are your questions about that Scripture? Find a time to sit quietly and meditate about the implications of that verse for your situation.

FASTING

Considering the alarming rate of obesity in the North American church, we might think fasting should be a mandatory spiritual discipline, beginning in the toddlers class. But fasting as a spiritual discipline is not primarily about controlling our weight or maintaining physical health. A spiritual commitment to be a good steward of the body God has given us could lead to fasting, but fasting is more than just going on a diet.

Fasting is the voluntary choice to abstain from eating all or certain foods for a set period of time. Other kinds of fasts include abstaining from sexual relations, favorite activities, hobbies, or entertainments;

or other practices for the sake of focusing our full attention on Christ. We will focus on abstaining from solid foods.

Fasting from food generally does not exclude the intake of fluids and should not include omitting prescribed medicines or the food necessary to take them. Those on prescribed diets or continuing medications that essentially control symptoms and make healthy life possible (people with diabetes, high blood pressure, seizures, and the like) should consult their physician before fasting.

The tradition of fasting began centuries before the birth of Christ. People have fasted as a way of expressing deeply felt emotions over spiritual transgressions, often sorrow or regret (see Joel 2:12–14), or of marking particularly memorable and often difficult events (see Zech. 7:2–5; 8:18–19). Over time people began to think of fasting as a way of gaining recognition from God and fellow believers. Jesus soundly rejected the notion that fasting itself had any particular merit (see Luke 18:9–14). He insisted that fasting and other acts of spiritual discipline were transactions between people and God, valuable only for the sake and in the course of an authentic relationship with God, not to impress God or others (see Matt. 6:1–18).

But Jesus clearly assumed his followers would fast. He said, "When you fast" (Matt. 6:16) not "If you fast." Christians choose to fast for many reasons. It is a way to elevate spiritual nourishment above matters of physical sustenance. It helps us give marked attention to the life, death, and resurrection of Jesus—especially at times of the year such as Lent. It focuses us on life with God in Christ over all other matters. It makes time available to practice the other spiritual disciplines. Fasting can also be a way of expressing solidarity with believers around the world who lack sufficient food or who are undergoing suffering.

Though fasting is not about striking a blow to one's body and making it a slave (see 1 Cor. 9:27), it is part of learning self-control, the essence of spiritual discipline. So, if our first reaction to the thought of fasting is that we could not possibly give up lunch or dinner, that reaction alone might indicate we could benefit from this discipline. If for no other reason, we could fast as an expression of our desire to "seek first [God's] kingdom" (Matt. 6:33).

Fasting involves more than simply refraining from eating. Eating occupies much of our time. The time we free up by fasting should be spent in prayer, meditation, study, or service in keeping with the goal of the fast. One might think that going without food would prove anything but helpful in focusing our attention beyond food. Surprisingly, this is usually not the case, especially when we become more experienced. Some people fast occasionally, others by the church calendar (Lent), and others on a regular basis (one meal or one day a week).

Have you ever fasted as a spiritual discipline? What was the goal of your fast? What did you learn about God or yourself?

BIBLE STUDY AND MEMORIZATION

Perhaps the most important reason spiritual discipline always includes Scripture study and memorization is that the Holy Spirit uses our study of the Word of God not only to inform us, but also to transform us into Christ's image. Scripture gives us the surest account of God's will, the clearest picture of the person of Jesus, and the most secure expectations for life in the Spirit.

By *study* we mean to include a variety of intentional readings of Scripture. Like the other disciplines, Bible study changes with the ebb and flow of life and with our growth in the faith. Sometimes we need to read rapidly and generally to get the big picture, covering book after book of the Bible in a survey sort of reading. This survey gives us an indispensable grasp of the whole story and helps us to situate ourselves within that story. At other times, we should pay extended attention to a single book such as Genesis, Matthew, or Romans, or a group of books, like the Pentateuch (the first five books of the Old Testament), the Gospels (the first four books of the New Testament), or the Epistles (the letters found in the New Testament). We can pause to dig deeply into specific, key passages in these books. As with other aspects of spiritual discipline, we are aiming here for the long haul in Bible study (see Ps. 1; 119:10; 2 Tim. 3:14–16).

Orientation for Bible Study

Study the Bible in units. Seek not just to know verses, but also to become familiar with the basic content and flow of books in their entirety. For instance, even though John 3:16 is a blessed promise, it seems even more wonderful when we understand it in the context of the rest of the gospel of John. Beginners would do well to start with Luke, Acts, Ephesians, and Genesis. This plan covers the life of Jesus, the history and teachings of the early church, and the Creator-Redeemer.

Basic equipment for Bible study includes a notebook for recording our insights (for example, using part of a journal). Recording our discoveries signals seriousness about our work. Scripture will be more understandable if we consult several versions of the Bible, including some reputable, contemporary paraphrases. A good concordance and Bible dictionary will also come in handy.

It is helpful to adopt a mind-set of first putting ourselves in the world of the ancient readers—a world without electricity, automobiles, computers, plastics, hypodermics, germs, viruses, or democracies as we know them. Then ponder how the Word they received applies to our situation today.

Directions for Bible Study

Entering Scripture study as a spiritual discipline is like getting on a subway loop. We can enter at any one of a number of points. But if we stay on the train, we will eventually stop at all the stations. The "stations" on the Scripture study loop are consecration, content, concept, Canon, and connection.

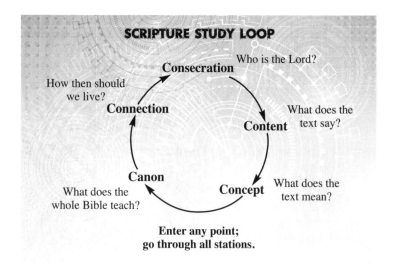

Life positions us to enter at any one of the different stations on the Scripture study loop. But no matter where we enter, lifelong Scripture study should pass through all the stops on the loop with all of Scripture.

Consecration. Who is Lord of our lives as we study? The best way to begin and end time in Scripture is by surrendering ourselves to

Christ, the Living Word, asking for teachable hearts and committing ourselves to apply what we learn.

Content. What exactly does the text say and how does it fit together? This is the time for observation. Start by seeing the overview of the book or chapter. Then move to the parts. For short books, give brief titles to the paragraphs; gather two to five paragraphs into segments and title these segments, and then give a title to the book as a whole. For longer books, move directly to giving titles to the chapters. Then gather chapters into divisions, and finally title the book. Observe the flow of thought in the book, passage, or paragraph. Does the unit have an introduction? What topics are introduced? Is there a turning point or a set of contrasting ideas? What questions are posed? How are themes developed to a climax? Spotting these elements will strengthen our grasp of the Word.

Concept. What does the text mean? Ask what the material meant to its early readers. At this stage, we begin to draw conclusions to interpret the text. For example, what did Paul mean by "the gospel" in Romans 1:16? How is it the "power of God that brings salvation"? How would Paul have defined the word *salvation*? Then look for answers to these questions by studying the book of Romans itself further and by consulting trusted resources.

Canon. What does the Bible as a whole teach on this issue? We can use a concordance, a topical Bible, or the cross-reference section of our Bible to locate other Bible passages that address the same issues as the passage we are studying. Listen to the conversation God has inspired on given topics in the Bible as a whole. The Spirit will enable us to discern how a given passage fits into that conversation and how it speaks cross-culturally to us today. If our conclusions are correct, the rest of Scripture will reinforce them.

Connection. How should we apply this text to our lives? Now that we have discovered what the Bible says and what it means, it is time to apply it to our situation. Asking questions can help here too. How does this teaching affirm, correct, and inform us? What sins should we confess? What specific choices should we make regarding our resources—property, time, money, reputation, health, influence, etc.? What affirmation or revision of faith or values should we make? We should think of applications both individually and corporately. In this lifelong process, the Word will shape us.

Memorization of Scripture

When we find a text that speaks powerfully to us, we should memorize it. This could be the key verse of a section or a passage that speaks pointedly to our current situations. Writing the text several times and speaking it as we write it will help us in the memory process. Many people find it helpful to post passages in prominent places such as on steering wheels, mirrors, exercise machines, workbenches, or any place conducive to review of the passage. Once we get comfortable memorizing short passages, we will be greatly blessed if we branch out to memorize short books such as Colossians or Philippians or famous passages like the Sermon on the Mount. If we set a pace such as a verse or paragraph a week, it is an easily achievable goal. The opening verse of each chapter in this book may help you begin memorizing.

What could you do to become more systematic in your study of the Word?

YOUR SPIRITUAL AMMUNITION

The spiritual disciplines of prayer, meditation, fasting, Bible study, and Scripture memorization provide our best ammunition against the Enemy. The effectiveness of the disciplines lies in the fact that they cultivate our relationship with the living Christ, just as the best defense against marital unfaithfulness is a satisfying relationship with our spouse. Our relationship with Christ actually constitutes the mainframe for the whole "weapons system" of the believer, without which "ammunition" proves useless or ineffective (see Eph. 6:10–20).

The disciplines are best practiced in a healthy Christian community. Our meaningful participation in a local church, regular study of God's Word in a Sunday school class or small group, plus fellowship with a group of friends who will hold us accountable is essential. This is our best ammunition against excess or error. The choices Paul encouraged as life habits of godliness in Colossians 3:15–17 are choices to be made by and in a group. It is wise to cultivate relationships with people who will support our life of prayer, Scripture study, memorization, meditation, fasting, and other Christian disciplines. These fellow believers can pray for and with us and keep us accountable, asking us the hard questions that will keep us honest and growing in the Lord.

Who in your life regularly practices these disciplines? What could you do to cultivate a supportive relationship with that person?

DEEPEN YOUR PASSION FOR GOD'S TRUTH

But seek first his kingdom and his righteousness,
and all these things will be given to you as well.

—Matthew 6:33

BIBLE BASICS

- Matthew 5:17–20

We know that salvation doesn't depend on our own good works. What do you think Jesus meant when he said our righteousness must surpass that of the Pharisees?

EXTREME RIGHTEOUSNESS

The Pharisees were the religious elite of Jesus' day. If you had lived in the first century, no doubt you would have greatly revered the Pharisees for their piety and scrupulous attention to the law of Moses. This religious group was so concerned about meticulously keeping the Ten Commandments and the other laws God gave to Moses (see Ex. 20–23) that they came up with their own set of rules to govern every aspect of daily life. Their intent to fully obey God was admirable, but something was missing. Jesus often condemned the Pharisees for their hypocrisy. They were following a list of rules, but in the process they forgot about love, justice, and compassion. They substituted outward righteous actions for the inward righteousness God required.

But how does that apply to us? Again, Jesus said in order to enter the kingdom of heaven our righteousness must surpass that of the Pharisees. Let's look at three key passages in the Bible that teach us about the righteousness God requires: the Ten Commandments, found in Exodus 20; the Great Commandment, found in Matthew 22:34–43; and the Sermon on the Mount, found in Matthew 5–7.

THE TEN COMMANDMENTS

Some 1,200 to 1,500 years before the time of Christ, God delivered his people (the Israelites) from bondage in Egypt through a series of plagues and by miraculously parting the Red Sea. He led them through the wilderness until they came to Mount Sinai. There, on the top of the mountain, God met with Moses for forty days and gave him the law—the Ten Commandments—along with many other regulations. These were not man-made laws; they were inscribed on tablets of stone by God's own finger (see Ex. 31:18). It was this law that set Israel apart from all the other nations. It was a law based on God's holiness and righteous requirements.

The people in the other nations had devised religions to appease their own lusts and appetites. Often the religions included debased sexual practices and drunken revelry. When people create their own religion, they devise a law that pleases them and is easy to keep. But God's law was completely different. It was based on his character and highlighted our complete inability to fulfill it in our own power. God revealed himself as holy and righteous, and he set forth his expectations for his people. They were to be holy and righteous because they belonged to him.

The verses that communicate the Ten Commandments are undoubtedly some of the best-known verses in the entire Bible. Jews, Christians, and Muslims, along with many other religious groups and governments, embrace them as the essence of morality.

Can you name all Ten Commandments from memory?

No Other Gods

The Lord God demands first place in our lives. He must be our highest priority, with no other gods ahead of him in our devotion and allegiance. What are some modern-day gods that vie for our attention and affection?

No Idols

Not only does God require that we honor him above all gods, but he also demands that we rid ourselves of all idols that compete for our devotion. God didn't want his people to merely add him to their list of deities or even place him at the top of the list. He expected them to worship him and him alone. After all, he is the only true God. Anything else is just a human-made mascot. Also, God didn't want the Israelites to make an earthly image of him and substitute human-made religion for a personal relationship with him.

Honor God's Name

God's name is an expression of his character. It is to be revered. By tossing his name around casually, or by using it as an expletive, we profane it and show contempt for his holiness and uniqueness. Have you ever found yourself saying, "Oh my God!" or "Thank God!" when you really weren't thinking about God at all? If we're caught in the habit of casually using God's name as filler for conversation, how can we begin to break that habit?

Remember the Sabbath Day

God gave us a day of rest so we wouldn't get caught up in the affairs of the world. The Sabbath is his gift to us to rejuvenate our physical and mental resources and refocus our minds on what is truly important in life. Read Mark 2:23–28; Colossians 2:16–17; and Romans 14:5. How can we honor the Sabbath without making it a legalistic ritual?

Honor Your Father and Mother

This doesn't need much explanation, but it does require some reflection. Is there a difference between obeying our parents and honoring them? Is it possible to obey our parents yet still dishonor them? Is it possible to honor our parents after we're grown without necessarily obeying their wishes?

Don't Murder

Don't intentionally and maliciously take another person's life.

Don't Commit Adultery

Any extramarital sexual relationship is strictly forbidden in Scripture. Many Christians pride themselves on being pure in this regard, yet they regularly sin by flirting with adultery. Read James 1:14–15. Where does sin begin? The outward act of adultery often begins when we fuel our desires by dwelling on impure thoughts, dressing or acting suggestively, or permitting exposure to pornography. How can we protect our hearts and minds from this destructive sin?

Don't Steal

This means not taking anything that doesn't belong to us. And we shouldn't conveniently forget to return something we borrowed. This command doesn't apply just to material possessions. Don't steal someone's ideas, reputation, self-worth, or influence.

Don't Lie

Don't lie. Tell "the truth, the whole truth, and nothing but the truth." There's no room for little white lies or gossip in the life of a true follower of God. Deception can be a powerful temptation. While we may technically be truthful in our statements to others, we must be careful that the outcome isn't deception or slander. Even if we think our lies won't hurt anyone, it ultimately hurts our relationship with God.

Don't Covet

We shouldn't fervently desire what doesn't belong to us or occupy our minds with schemes of how to obtain our neighbor's possessions. We must watch out if we are filled with jealousy over another's achievements or success (and plot to overthrow him or her or take the credit). If we put material possessions, prestige, or power above God, we are breaking the first commandment. In our materialistic society, how can we keep from constantly desiring the newest and best and feeling deprived when we don't get it?

Indicate which commandments represent a personal struggle for you. Choose the one commandment you fear breaking. Write it in your journal and list three specific actions you can do—or not do—to help you remain obedient.

THE GREAT COMMANDMENT

A Pharisee, who was an expert in the law, asked Jesus to name the greatest commandment in the law. Jesus said, "'Love the Lord your God with all your heart and with all your soul and with all your mind.' This is the first and greatest commandment. And the second is like it: 'Love your neighbor as yourself.' All the Law and the Prophets hang on these two commandments" (Matt. 22:37–40).

Do you find these two listed in the Ten Commandments? The answer is yes. Jesus said the entire Law and the Prophets hang on our love for God and our love for others. It is easy to become so focused on outward compliance with the Ten Commandments that we miss the inner foundation of love. The Pharisees certainly did, and they were supposed to be the experts! Read the story of the rich young man in Mark 10:17–22. He had meticulously kept the Ten Commandments, but he lacked one thing, the foundation of love.

Most of us seem to struggle with either loving God or loving others. Either we instinctively love God and struggle to love others, or we are so concerned with loving others that we fail to show proper love and respect for God. We need to honestly examine our lives before God. We'll never grow as disciples and become all God wants us to be unless we honestly confront our sins and ask for forgiveness and grace to live a balanced life.

THE SERMON ON THE MOUNT

Some people think there is no correlation between the Old Testament and the New, or they believe the New Testament makes the Old Testament obsolete. They couldn't be further from the truth! In Matthew 5:17, Jesus said, "Do not think that I have come to abolish the Law or the Prophets; I have not come to abolish them but to fulfill them." Jesus spoke these words in his Sermon on the Mount, recorded in Matthew 5–7. In this memorable sermon delivered to his disciples near the Sea of Galilee, Jesus set forth the ethical laws of the kingdom he came to inaugurate. He shared God's requirements with them in a new and fresh way that paralleled the Ten Commandments God had given centuries before. He also addressed some of the 613 laws of the Pharisees. Jesus came to fulfill the law and to make it possible for us to live righteously by his power. He came to show us true righteousness (a righteousness that far exceeds that of the Pharisees). This is what God had expected all along.

Read the Sermon on the Mount in Matthew 5–7, and note especially the Ten Commandments from Exodus 20 that Jesus amplified. Jesus didn't specifically mention all of the Commandments, such as honoring your parents or keeping the Sabbath holy, but he did give guidelines that apply to them.

Jesus taught this sermon to his disciples. Disciples were learners, those who followed their master closely—listening to his teachings, memorizing his words, and copying his behavior. We, too, are called to be Jesus' disciples, not casual or occasional followers. Let's look more closely at the Sermon on the Mount to see what we can learn about becoming more like Christ—about becoming true disciples. (Be sure to read the indicated passage from Matthew before the comments that follow.)

The Qualities of a Disciple: Matthew 5:3–12

This passage is known as the Beatitudes because of the repetition of the word *blessed*. Here Jesus listed eight qualities that should characterize a true disciple's life. They're not listed so we can choose the ones we want to possess. We're expected to display all of them. As we seek to develop these qualities in our lives, Jesus said we will be blessed. To be blessed means to possess an inner happiness, contentment, and deep satisfaction. And it can be achieved only by cultivating these eight qualities.

Be Poor in Spirit. We do this by ridding ourselves of all pride and self-sufficiency (see Luke 18:9–14 for a good illustration). We must recognize that all our human righteousness is worthless and we depend totally on God's righteousness.

Be Mournful. Mourning is a passionate lament for a loved one, a sorrow that penetrates the soul. It implies great compassion for others (see Rom. 12:15).

Be Gentle and Meek. The original term used here means strength under control, calmness in the midst of pressure, or gracious courtesy. Think for a moment about Jesus' life because he was a perfect example of gentleness and meekness.

Notice the promise for those who are meek: "They will inherit the earth" (Matt. 5:5). How different this is from the world's philosophy! The world believes meek people will be stepped on and end up last, but Jesus assured us the meek will win in the end.

Be Spiritually Hungry and Thirsty. This is a voracious appetite for righteousness, a passionate drive for justice, and the relentless pursuit of God. We tend to become complacent and satisfied with our own level of spirituality and apathetic toward sin and injustice in the world around us. But if we are true disciples, we will strive for holiness and righteousness both in ourselves and our society. Our love for God and others will compel us.

Did you notice the promise for those who hunger and thirst for righteousness? They will be filled or completely satisfied. The word used here for "filled" is the same word used to describe those who witnessed the miracle of the loaves and fish in Matthew 14. Jesus fed five thousand men, plus women and children, with only five loaves of bread and two fish. Yet there were twelve basketfuls left over. Verse 20 reports, "They all ate and were satisfied." That means they were completely full and content. God is always gracious to give us more of himself when we seek more of him. If we draw near to God, he will always draw near to us.

Be Merciful. Mercy is active concern for those who are hurting. It is the act of giving what is not deserved. It is getting personally involved and offering help. Pity is not enough; being merciful takes effort. Read Matthew 25:31–46; 1 John 3:17; and James 2:15–16 for some ideas about how to show mercy to others.

Be Pure in Heart. This refers to purity in our motives and intentions. It means there is no hatred, dissension, jealousy, or bitterness lurking in the recesses of our hearts. Does this sound impossible? It is, without the grace and power of the Holy Spirit working in and through us. The promise for those who are pure in heart is that "they will see God" (Matt. 5:8). Purity in heart (holiness) brings us close to his heart. Our eyes are opened so we can truly "see" him, both now and for eternity.

Be a Peacemaker. This does not mean we should avoid conflicts or compromise our convictions to appease others. It is more than being merely relaxed or easygoing. Peacemakers are at peace with themselves and work to settle quarrels rather than to start or advance them. Can you see why peacemakers are called "children of God" (v. 9)?

They stand out in the crowd and everyone recognizes them as godly. They work to restore broken relationships.

Be Glad in Persecution. The key to rejoicing in the midst of persecution is realizing that our reward is in heaven. We don't live each day for temporal, earthly reward or satisfaction, but for a reward that lasts forever.

Notice that these eight qualities don't lead to prosperity; they lead to blessedness. When we live the way God expects us to live, we find a deep, abiding joy and contentment that is far greater than any material possessions or pleasures the world has to offer.

The deeper we grow in our commitment to becoming true disciples of Christ, the more we will possess these qualities and desire the rewards Jesus mentioned. We are making progress when we find that we want God more than we want something material. We are on the right track when we long to be called children of God more than we long for esteem from others. Then we will be the kind of Christians God has called and enables us to be.

As you read the descriptions of these beatitudes, which quality seems most lacking in your life? Name one practical thing you can do to cultivate that quality.

The Influence of a Disciple: Matthew 5:13–16

Jesus compared a true disciple's influence to salt and light. Although salt is common today, it was so precious in Jesus' day that it was often given to soldiers as payment for wages. The phrase, "he isn't worth his salt," and the English word *salary* both come from that practice. Consider how important salt was and still is. It enhances the flavor of everything it touches, but if we use too much it ruins our food. Salt serves no purpose if it stays in the shaker, and salt should never draw attention to itself. True disciples are to act like salt in the world. As we stand for truth, our words and actions have a redeeming effect on the world around us. Our acts of compassion make the world a better, more livable place.

Our influence is also like light. Light exposes hidden things, illuminates our pathway, brings cheer, stimulates growth, and preserves life. Jesus said we shouldn't be secret Christians. We should let our light shine so others can benefit by coming into contact with our authentic, committed Christian example. We lead lives that are different from those who don't know Christ. In addition to the verbal testimony we give, our lives become shining examples of what God's love can do. That positive difference causes even nonbelievers to praise God. In that way, the "light" of our lives can lead others to acknowledge Christ.

How can you bless the people around you by being salt and light to them?

The Character of a Disciple: Matthew 5:17–48

Jesus taught that our righteousness must surpass the righteousness of the Pharisees in order for us to have eternal life. If we could simply follow a list of rules and make it to heaven, we wouldn't need Jesus at all. But think about it for a moment. Wouldn't it be easier if we had a checklist to mark off every day? Read the Bible. Check. Pray before meals. Check. Go to church. Check. While those things are important, our characters and motives are of greatest concern. What Christ is doing *in* us is far more important than what we are doing *for* Christ. In this next section of the Sermon on the Mount, Jesus contrasted the Pharisees' external interpretation of the law with the internal principles that should govern our lives as disciples. He gave six examples, each following the formula, "You have heard that it was said . . . but I tell you . . ."

Obey from the Heart. Jesus cited two specific Commandments: Do not murder and do not commit adultery. But he explained that love for others, not rules, should govern our behavior. So he discussed the obvious corollaries: do not be angry and do not lust. We are not to allow anger toward others to fester in us. Nor should we belittle others. It's up to us to make amends if someone is angry with us. We are responsible to make sure we're not causing someone else to sin, either by allowing them to remain angry with us or through divorce (see also Rom. 14:13–21).

Pursue Inward Integrity. Jesus said we should gouge out our eyes or cut off our hands if they are causing us to sin. Surely Jesus didn't mean this literally! Or did he? He wants us to realize that God hates sin, and we must use drastic measures to deal with it (see Hab. 1:13; Rom. 6:23; Heb. 12:14). Because he knew the consequences of our sins, he urged us to pay any price to remain spotless. God has always demanded that his people reflect his character. We're to be holy because he is holy.

Our integrity should be beyond reproach. Jesus used the example of keeping oaths to illustrate this point. The people of his day had developed an elaborate system of taking oaths. They had to swear by something for their word to be credible at all. It was a lot like when children say, "Cross my heart and hope to die." It was proof one was telling the truth. For true disciples, every word that comes from our mouths should be true and trustworthy. Our *yes* should always mean yes and our *no* should always mean no. People shouldn't have to second-guess us or wonder if we're twisting our words to deceive them. This is a matter of integrity and indicates what's in our hearts, "for the mouth speaks what the heart is full of" (Matt. 12:34).

Go the Extra Mile. Most people today are concerned about their rights, especially people who live in North America. We claim the right to be compensated if we're hurt, live or work anywhere we want, say anything we want, do anything we want, and be heard. True disciples understand that in Christ we have no rights. We give them all up to follow Jesus, just as he gave up his rights when he was here on earth (the right to a fair trial, the right to respect). First Corinthians 6:19–20 tells us we don't even belong to ourselves; we were bought at a price. Christ bought us by his shed blood on the cross. He owns us; we're his slaves; we don't have any rights.

Jesus told us that, as true disciples, we should turn the other cheek, go the extra mile, love our enemies, and pray for those who persecute us. This goes against our very nature. And it all comes back to loving God and loving others. It's only when God's love flows through us that we are able to love others in a way that is unnatural to the rest of the world. We give up any right to vengeance or vindication. In our love, we become perfect, as our heavenly Father is perfect.

What do you need to cut out of your life in order to deepen your level of integrity as a disciple?

The Lifestyle of a Disciple: Matthew 6:1–18

Do you feel overwhelmed by the standard Jesus has called you to? Do you think it's impossible to live up to it? No doubt the disciples felt the same way! At this point, they might have even been calculating how they were going to change or what they were going to start doing. Or maybe they felt so overwhelmed they didn't know where to begin. So Jesus continued by explaining how to live as a disciple, warning about pitfalls and offering encouragement in the process.

Do Acts of Righteousness. Jesus began by warning against doing our righteous acts before people. He didn't say we're not to do them at all, because righteous acts are a natural result of a righteous heart.

Rather, he listed three specific acts of righteousness we are expected to perform as disciples: giving to the needy, praying, and fasting. These good deeds are not ways to earn salvation or favor from God, but they are the overflow of our love for him and others and should be part of our lives. God expects us to do acts of righteousness.

Notice just a few of the instructions Jesus gave on prayer: It should be sincere and not just a routine repetition of words. We should pray for his will to be done on earth as well as for our daily needs. We shouldn't ask God to forgive us if we're not willing to forgive others.

Serve the God Who Sees in Secret. Although the Pharisees originally meant well, in time they became conceited about their spirituality. They did their righteous acts in a way that was calculated to attract public attention and honor to themselves. They wanted everyone to think they were extremely pious. But we shouldn't do that. Our motive in doing good should be to receive our answer and reward from God, not from people. Jesus pointed out that it is hypocritical to do good deeds without the proper motivation. We should always ask ourselves, "Who gets the credit?"

Expect Reward from God. Actually, the Pharisees received a reward for their good works. They received exactly what they were looking for—acclaim from the people who observed them, but they received nothing more. When we do our acts of righteousness in secret with the proper motivation, we also receive a reward, one that is heavenly and spiritual. Don't be discouraged in living out the righteous life as a disciple. God will certainly bless us for putting our love for him and others into action.

Can you think of an act of kindness you could do for someone this week? Write it in your journal, and then do it without letting anyone know what you have done.

The Priorities of a Disciple: Matthew 6:19–34

When addressing priorities, Jesus spoke about money because, for many people, it is their prime motivation in life and their highest priority. In our capitalistic society, most things revolve around money. Isn't money the primary determinant in many of our decisions? In this passage, Jesus taught us that earthly treasures are fleeting. We can lose them in a moment. And in the end, they really don't satisfy our deepest longings anyway. They are often just a substitute or distraction from our real goals.

But we must be careful. Earthly riches or possessions can easily capture our affections. One of the most poignant principles in all of Scripture is this: "Where your treasure is, there your heart will be also" (v. 21). Let's think about this. When someone spends a lot of money on a new car, he will love that car. He'll take extra time to clean and maintain it. If someone devotes a lot of time to a hobby, that too will capture her heart. It will be what she thinks about when she lies down at night and when she gets up in the morning. Jesus' point was that whatever we spend our greatest energy on will capture our hearts. Wherever we place our "treasure" (and it's not always money), our hearts are sure to follow. And, consequently, our devotion to God will shrink. We can't serve two masters. Our highest priority should be Jesus and serving him. That's what God stated in the first two of the Ten Commandments. Our love for him must far exceed our love for anything else.

For many Christians, our preoccupation with money or earthly possessions has more to do with need than want. We're worried we won't be able to provide for our children or have the money to make ends meet. But we don't need to worry. Jesus promises that we are of great value to God (see Matt. 6:8; 10:30; John 3:16). He loves us, will always care for us, and will provide everything we need if our priorities are right. Whenever we seek God and his righteousness first, he will take care of everything else.

Describe an instance when God provided for you.

The Guidelines for a Disciple: Matthew 7:1–29

Set Your Own Life in Order First. As we've worked through this chapter, you probably thought of many applications for people you know: spouse, parent, or maybe even pastor. But every word of the Sermon on the Mount was written for us first. Jesus pointed this out to his listeners. He said we should correct our own big faults before we judge others and try to correct their little faults. We should continually meditate on God's Word, asking God to show us what we must change in our own lives.

Count on God's Supply. If we feel inadequate or defeated, we can remember that God will give us the righteous life we desire. All we have to do is ask, seek, and knock. God wants us to be righteous and holy even more than we want it. And he has the power to make it so. He wants to fill us with his love so we are able to fully love him and others. But we must first want to have that love, and we have to ask for it.

Enter at the Narrow Gate. We are responsible to choose the narrow road that Jesus pointed out to us. Our goal shouldn't be to see how little we can do and still be considered disciples. We need to get as close to God as possible no matter if anyone else joins us or not.

Choose Wisely Whom to Follow. False prophets abound. Many people will try to shipwreck our faith and lead us astray. Jesus described them as wolves in sheep's clothing. They may say and do impressive things, and even perform miracles, but their fruit will always give them away. In Galatians 5:22–23, the fruit of the Spirit is described as:

love, joy, peace, forbearance (patience), kindness, goodness, faithfulness, gentleness, and self-control. We should inspect fruit before we take a bite! Is the person we want to follow obedient to the commands in God's Word? Is he or she doing God's will?

Do you think Jesus gave us a lot of practical suggestions for growing in our spiritual life? He didn't! Nothing he said in the Sermon on the Mount was a suggestion. Furthermore, God gave us the Ten Commandments, not the "Ten Suggestions." Jesus knew that the only way to find true fulfillment, satisfaction, and contentment was by becoming true disciples. Blessings come when we put our Christianity into practice by living out the law of love.

After he recorded the Sermon on the Mount, Matthew wrote, "The crowds were amazed at [Jesus'] teaching, because he taught as one who had authority, and not as their teachers of the law" (Matt. 7:28–29). Jesus' words had authority, because he spoke exactly what God gave him to speak (see John 7:16; 14:10). You can purchase many books like this one that will help you grow in your Christian walk, but no other book can do for you what the Word of God can. God's Word has authority and power. It will change your life.

What do you sense God telling you to do as a next step toward becoming more like Jesus?

DEVELOP A BIBLICAL ORTHODOXY

—— 🔲 ——

Watch your life and doctrine closely. Persevere in them, because
if you do, you will save both yourself and your hearers.

—1 Timothy 4:16

BIBLE BASICS

- 1 Timothy 4:7–16
- 2 Peter 3:18

How do you know what you believe is really the truth?

THE IMPORTANCE OF A BIBLICAL VIEW

Mohammed Atta was an educated and devoted Muslim from one
of the wealthiest nations in the Middle East. On September 11, 2001,
he piloted an American Airlines jet as it crashed into one of the World

Trade Center towers in New York City. His religious mentor promised him that for his efforts he would be welcomed into heaven's glory with a reward of seventy virgins.

On December 7, 1977, Eldon McCorkhill and Linda Cummings had a few drinks in a bar in Redlands, California, and talked about their beliefs in an afterlife. Linda told her friend that she was finally convinced of the reality of reincarnation. A spirited debate continued all the way back to McCorkhill's apartment. Once there, he pulled a loaded pistol out of his drawer and handed it to her. "If you believe in this, let's see what you'll come back as," he challenged. Linda took the gun, pointed it to her head and pulled the trigger.

In January 1956, the Auca Indians of Ecuador martyred Nate Saint, Jim Elliot, and three fellow missionaries. Nine years after this brutal slaying, the gospel of Mark was published in the Auca language. Among the many Aucas who turned to Christ were the six men who had killed the missionaries. Nate's sister, Rachel Saint, led the translation team God used to reach the Aucas. She refused to shrink from Christ's call to reach the very people who had brutally killed her brother.

What do these three stories have in common? They are stories of sincerely devoted people with deeply held, though widely divergent, beliefs that led them to take specific, faith-led action steps. In dramatic fashion, they illustrate the truth that what we believe makes a difference! What we believe about God's character and human nature—not to mention other theological topics—ultimately shapes our attitudes and actions. In the end, we all live out what we believe. If our beliefs are faulty, they will eventually lead to faulty behavior. Knowing that, the apostle Paul admonished his young disciple Timothy, "Watch your life and doctrine closely" (1 Tim. 4:16).

Unfortunately, many believers neglect the study of the doctrines that undergird their faith. They believe, but their grasp of what they believe—not to mention why they believe it—remains sketchy at best. These believers are hard pressed to articulate a thoroughly biblical worldview or even core Christian beliefs.

The word *doctrine* sounds boring. Yet most people find that learning the foundational truths of the Christian faith is anything but boring. Upon discovering core biblical belief, new believers commonly respond with statements such as:

- "I thought all religions believed basically the same thing. But now I see that biblical Christianity is truly unique."
- "Theology and doctrine always seemed stale and boring. But now I see how relevant these beliefs are to my life."
- "My faith has become so much stronger as I have grown in my understanding of what the Bible teaches."

Let's take a look at some key doctrines.

THE AUTHORITY OF THE BIBLE

How do we know what the truth is? What is our measure, standard, or authority? People have developed three basic answers to these questions. Some people insist that we can never really know truth. Others say that human reason is the final authority for testing our truth assertions. People who believe this are secular humanists. Human reason is limited, faulty, and changeable in response to new discoveries, fads, and cultural pressures.

The third and best alternative grows out of our faith that the almighty God has revealed truth to us, and the Bible, God's Word, constitutes his written revelation to us. Indeed, the Bible claims this of itself. The Bible says, "All Scripture is God-breathed and is useful for teaching, rebuking, correcting and training in righteousness" (2 Tim. 3:16). Christianity claims that forty men wrote the Bible but the Holy Spirit guided them so precisely that what they wrote was not the wisdom of men but the verbally inspired Word of God (see 2 Tim. 3:16; 2 Pet. 1:20–21). This revelation, the Bible, possesses an authority for faith and practice that surpasses human reason, church tradition, and even human experience. This is not to say that reason, tradition, and experience are not vital to spirituality. They have their place, but the final authority for truth is God's revealed Word, the Bible.

It's not up to us to decide what God is like. Only he can tell us what he is like and what he requires of us. He has revealed himself to us through his Word, and we must align our beliefs about him with his revelation. Similarly with every aspect of doctrine, our faith is not merely the product of human reason, the church's teaching, or even our own experiences. We look to the Bible as our source for revealed truth, and we subject all other standards to the test of biblical authority.

But doesn't every religion have its own holy book? What makes the Bible a superior revelation to Islam's Quran or Hinduism's Vedas? The full answer to these questions deserves much more space than we have here. But a study of comparative religions reveals how uniquely the Bible is grounded in historical reality and how the answers it provides to the key questions of life ring true to the way life is and the way people are. Both the internal witness found in the Bible and the external witness found in history, archaeology, and other disciplines support the Bible's claim to be a "God-breathed" book. (To explore in depth this matter of the sufficiency and full authority of Scripture, look up these passages: Ps. 19:7; Matt. 5:17–19; Acts 17:2, 11; 2 Tim. 3:15–17; 2 Pet. 1:19–21; Rev. 22:8–19.)

Why is the Bible more reliable than opinion?

THE BIBLICAL VIEW OF GOD

While it is true that God is spirit and cannot be reduced to picture-form, the Bible paints a remarkable picture of the nature and character of the one, true, living God. Among his many attributes are those that reflect the infinite side of his being. He is eternal, unlimited in power, wisdom, and goodness. He is the creator and preserver of all that exists (see Gen. 1:1; Col. 1:16–17). Splendor, majesty, and glory characterize his being. He is a holy God, pure and perfect in every way.

Yet this infinite God is also intensely personal. He is a God of holy love. James 1:17 says, "Every good and perfect gift is from above, coming down from the Father of the heavenly lights, who does not change like shifting shadows." Righteousness, justice, mercy, and grace make up the wonderful character of God, who relates to us as a heavenly Father. The God of the Bible is revealed as the sovereign ruler of the universe.

Unique to this biblical view of God is the Trinity, or tri-unity, of his being—one God who exists externally in three persons. This community of holy love at the center of the Godhead is one of the great mysteries. The Bible consistently affirms that there is one living and true God (see Deut. 6:4), yet the Father is God, Jesus Christ the Son is God, and the Holy Spirit is also God.

The clearest and most personal revelation God has given us of himself came with the incarnation of God in the person of Jesus Christ. While Jesus was fully man, he was also fully God. His life, from conception by the Holy Spirit and virgin birth to the miracles he performed and the sinless life he led, to his sacrificial death on a cross, triumphant resurrection from the dead, and ascension into heaven, gives evidence that he is the divine Messiah.

God continues to work in our world through the Holy Spirit's ongoing ministry. Of the same essential nature, majesty, and glory as the Father and the Son, the Holy Spirit administers God's grace to us. His ministry includes awakening, convicting, regenerating, enlightening, sanctifying, assuring, preserving, guiding, and enabling those who respond in faith.

This biblical view of God differs radically from that found in other religions. Compared to the pantheism of Hinduism or even the portrait of Allah found in the Islamic Quran, the God of the Bible is unique and marvelous. We can only stand in amazement at the glory of this God who is both infinitely beyond us and yet intensely personal toward us.

What is the role of each member of the Trinity? Pause to worship God and to thank him for revealing himself to you.

THE BIBLICAL VIEW OF HUMANITY

A true faith must account for both the wonder and wickedness of human beings. According to Genesis 1:27, God created human beings in his image to enjoy a love relationship with him and with their fellow image-bearers. Everything that is good about us — from the capabilities of the human mind to the kindnesses we show others—can be traced back to the image of God in us. God created us to live in community with him in a relationship of mutual knowing, loving, serving, and celebrating. Similarly, God created us to live in community with one another, where we can know and be known, love and be loved, serve and be served, and celebrate and be celebrated.

As God's image-bearers, we are endowed with the capacity to make moral choices. Both the Bible and secular history record the story of human race's rebellion against God's will. The Bible defines sin both as actions that violate God's law and as a condition that has corrupted human nature. We are born into this world with a sinful nature that accounts for the inclination toward evil that plagues us all. We are not good or godly by nature. As a result, we fall short of the glory of a holy God (Rom. 3:23). Our sin not only wreaks havoc in our relationships with one another, but it also makes us deserving of God's righteous judgment. We are spiritually dead and in desperate need of salvation.

In many ways, the Bible gives us both good and bad news about humanity. It is good news to discover that we are created in God's image and thus all human life possesses dignity, value, and remarkable capacity. But our moral and spiritual depravity is bad news. Our condition is hopeless apart from God's intervention. The good news is that God in his great mercy and love has not left us to ourselves. John Wesley coined the term *prevenient grace* to describe the grace God freely bestowed upon all people, enabling all to be saved.

What great purposes provide meaning for your life?

THE BIBLICAL VIEW OF SALVATION

At the center of the Christian gospel is the work Jesus accomplished when he laid down his life on the cross. The cross has become the most visible symbol of the Christian faith because it plays a central role in God's great plan of salvation. That plan had to solve the grand dilemma of how a sinful race, lost and helpless, could be reconciled to a holy God. The answer to that dilemma could not come from any mere human. But at the cross, God released his gracious forgiveness and pardon in a way that did not violate his holiness, righteousness, and justice (see Rom. 3:24–26). Christ offered himself as the perfect sacrifice for the sins of the world and thereby made his perfect righteousness available to humanity.

Many people stumble over the Bible's insistence that "there is no other name under heaven given to mankind by which we must be saved" (Acts 4:12). But the reality is apart from God's grace that offered Christ as a sacrificial atonement for sin, there is no hope for our salvation. Salvation is not something we can earn by our good works or religious practices. Salvation is a gift of God's grace.

We gain access to this grace through faith (see Eph. 2:8; Rom. 5:1–2). Saving faith is an important, but often misunderstood, responsibility that God has placed before every person. It is not merely an intellectual conviction. James 2:19 informs us that even demons believe that there is one God, but that intellectual assent does not save them. Saving faith leads us to repent by turning away from sin and sinfulness and turning to Jesus Christ by receiving him as Savior and Lord.

Several things happen when we take this step of repentance and faith. Here is a list of some of the great theological terms associated with our salvation:

- *Justification* is a judicial term that involves the pardon of sin and the establishment of a righteous relationship with the holy God (see Acts 13:38–39; Rom. 1:16–17; Phil. 3:9).
- *Regeneration* is the work of the Holy Spirit that creates new spiritual life in people who have been dead in sin (see John 3:3–8; 2 Cor. 5:17; Eph. 2:4–5).
- *Adoption* signifies that someone who was outside of God's family has been adopted as his child (see Rom. 8:14–15; Gal. 4:5–7).
- *Assurance* is the work of the Holy Spirit now residing in us to witness to our spirits that we are children of God (see Rom. 8:16).

These precious gifts belong to people who cross the line of faith and become followers of Jesus Christ. Thus begins the great adventure of leading the spiritual life.

Why is faith in Jesus the only way to be saved?

THE BIBLICAL VIEW OF THE SPIRITUAL LIFE

Coming to Christ marks the beginning of a new life in the Spirit (see Rom. 8:9; Gal. 5:16). It is important to remember that our good works are *not* the basis of our salvation. We are saved by grace, not by our own good works. But the saved person finds that saving faith leads to a new desire and an ability to do the good works that God created his people to perform (see Eph. 2:10).

This is not to say that we live perfectly sinless lives. The reality is that the same free will that was exercised in sinful ways prior to coming to Christ can still be exercised in sinful ways after our conversion. The Bible warns us to guard our lives because in this fallen world, it will always be possible to fall into sinful patterns that can wreak devastating consequences in our lives. When we do sin, the Holy Spirit prompts us to confession, forgiveness, and restoration (see 1 John 1:8–9). However, it is our responsibility to choose to respond submissively to his prompting.

The Holy Spirit's work in the believer goes beyond the conviction of sin. God desires to set us free from the power of sin so we can live in full harmony with his perfect love. This work of the Spirit is called *sanctification*, which refers to the process God uses to transform our sinful character into conformity with his holy character (see Heb. 13:12; 1 Pet. 1:15). The goal of this process is to make us like Christ in our character and conduct. All the resources of the kingdom are now available to make holiness both an attainable goal and a present possibility for every believer.

The work of sanctification in a believer goes through several stages.

Initial sanctification begins the moment we give our lives to Christ. Every true believer receives the precious gift of the indwelling Holy Spirit. This initial sanctification leads to a gradual process of spiritual growth in grace. During these early stages of growth, we experience both the joys of the Spirit's influence as well as the internal conflict with our sinful nature and residual pre-Christian habits. The inconsistency of this internal conflict, compounded by the ongoing influence of the world, the flesh, and the Devil, can often discourage us. We grow tired of living in part-time victory and spiritual weakness.

As we read the New Testament, we discover a resounding call to continue to grow in the process of sanctification, but we also find a call to a deeper consecration. Romans 12:1 urges Christians to "offer [their] bodies as a living sacrifice, holy and pleasing to God." This process of sanctification leads to the crisis moment when we consecrate our lives completely to God. John Wesley called this experience *entire sanctification*. What is most significant about the experience of entire sanctification is the work that the Holy Spirit does in response to our act of consecration. This work involves a deep cleansing of the totally yielded heart, a deep infusion of the perfect love of God, and a deep empowering for holy living and effective service.

Some have misconstrued the idea of entire sanctification to mean a life without the possibility of sin. While such a state would be wonderful, Wesley recognized that we still live in a fallen world. While we may live without *willfully* disobeying the known will of God, we will always be subject to temptation and will continue to struggle with our infirmities and weaknesses. Still, the Holy Spirit enables us to grow in obedience to God's will and to produce the fruit of the Spirit in our lives (Gal. 5:22–23). Spiritual growth continues even after entire sanctification, making holiness a lifelong experience.

In addition to his work of sanctification, the Holy Spirit gives spiritual gifts to help us live the spiritual life. Actually, the preeminent gift of the Spirit is the Holy Spirit himself. He also gives spiritual abilities that uniquely equip us for effective service as members of the body of Christ. The most comprehensive lists of these spiritual gifts are found in Romans 12 and 1 Corinthians 12. The discovery, development, and deployment of our spiritual gifts help us to find our niche in the ministry of the church and can become a source of deep fulfillment and fruitfulness in the spiritual life.

What deeper work do you sense the Holy Spirit desiring to do in you?

THE BIBLICAL VIEW OF THE CHURCH

A biblical view of the church has little to do with the buildings, services, worship styles, or committees of a particular congregation. Local churches are a visible manifestation of the church that is composed of everyone who believes in Jesus Christ and acknowledges him as the founder and Head of the church. The church's mission is to carry on Christ's work until he returns. That work includes evangelism, discipleship, fellowship, and worship. These biblical purposes should shape the priorities of every local church.

It is not enough to profess faith in Christ. The New Testament clearly indicates that as people came to Christ in the first century, they were immediately enfolded into a local body of believers. Throughout history God has raised up a variety of churches and movements to fulfill the biblical purposes of the church and to reach the variety of people who need Christ. Most Protestant churches believe that Christ ordained water baptism and the Lord's Supper as a sacramental means of grace to those who participate by faith. The Lord's Supper reminds us of the death of Christ and the renewal of the life that is found only in his grace. Likewise, baptism is an outward sign of an inward work of grace. By this step of obedience, new believers declare their faith in Christ.

What does it take for a church to become a biblically functioning community?

THE BIBLICAL VIEW OF LAST THINGS

The question of where we are going and what the future holds is an important part of our theology. The Bible provides some clear indications regarding the way this world will come to an end. Christ promised that he would personally return to earth to mark the end of this age (see Matt. 16:27; John 14:3; Acts 1:11). His coming would signal the final and complete triumph over evil (see Rev. 19:11–21). This coming would be followed by the resurrection of the dead and the judgment of humanity (see Rev. 20:5–14).

A biblical worldview affirms that there is an eternal destiny awaiting us all. The Bible paints a glorious picture of heaven as a place of blessedness for all those who choose the salvation God provides through Jesus Christ. Likewise, the Bible paints an agonizing picture of hell as a place of everlasting misery and separation from God for all who reject this great salvation.

We are to live in the light of these eternal realities. Our hope is this: We don't just live for today because our destiny is the incredible kingdom that belongs to our holy God. This hope spurs us on to lead holy lives and reach out to a lost and dying world. We would be most foolish to face eternity without a Savior and sacrifice the glory of heaven for the cares and trinkets of this world. We live every day between these two eternal destinies.

LIFELONG LEARNING

This chapter has presented a brief summary of basic Christian beliefs. Don't stop there. Go further. Dig deeper. Build your theology on the firm foundation of God's Word. What we believe really does make a difference!

How would your behavior change if you knew Jesus would return today?

NURTURE FAMILIES OF DISCIPLES

— □ —

Walk in the way of love, just as Christ loved us and gave himself
up for us as a fragrant offering and sacrifice to God.

—Ephesians 5:2

BIBLE BASICS

- Genesis 1:27–28
- Ephesians 4:32 — 5:3

From these Scriptures, list several key words that describe an ideal
family life. What values do you consider important for a family?

FAMILY IS GOD'S IDEA

The origin of the family dates back to Adam and Eve. God created the
family in the garden of Eden. It was his way of saying, "This is the best

way for you to live." Family is the basic unit of society and the guarantee of our future.

God created a beautiful world for Adam to live in. It overflowed with delicious fruits, colorful flowers, and a variety of animals. And Adam had work to do, tending the garden and naming the animals. Who wouldn't be happy in that paradise? Yet even the garden of Eden was not enough for Adam. He was lonely for human companionship.

God observed Adam and remarked, "It is not good for the man to be alone. I will make a helper suitable for him" (Gen. 2:18). Then he created Eve to be a wife for Adam, and the first family began.

The Purpose of Family

When God created Adam and Eve, he established some essential truths about family life. This first family, one man and one woman, was created to tend the garden together and to bear children (see Gen. 1:26, 28). Their partnership was not simply for their own fulfillment. It had a purpose. Also, God wanted to relate to this couple. They were created for fellowship with their Creator. God stipulated that those who would enter into marriage would leave their parents and become attached to their spouses (see Gen. 2:24).

The Gift of Gender

If you look beyond the moral character of each person, you may observe that men and women, by their nature, are each like God in certain ways. This gives new meaning to the words, "God created mankind in his own image, in the image of God he created them; male and female he created them" (Gen. 1:27). In some ways, the image of God is more fully reflected in Adam and Eve together than in either one of them individually.

76

Equality of the Sexes

The New Testament adds to our understanding of God's plan for marriage. While men and women may serve different roles in the family, Scripture insists that we look beyond gender differences to affirm that men and women are completely equal before God. Paul wrote, "There is neither Jew nor Gentile, neither slave nor free, nor is there male and female, for you are all one in Christ Jesus" (Gal. 3:28). Peter said, "Husbands, in the same way be considerate as you live with your wives, and treat them with respect . . . as heirs with you of the gracious gift of life" (1 Pet. 3:7). After all, Jesus had already taught that in heaven people will not be married, for current gender roles will be transcended (see Matt. 22:30).

God's Blessing on Marriage

After God created Adam and Eve as the first family, he blessed them and pronounced that all he had made was "very good" (Gen. 1:31). Marriage and the family have God's explicit blessing and approval.

All of us, regardless of marital status, are part of families, and we can model the characteristics of a godly home. Let's learn more about those characteristics and what we can do to develop strong marriages and families.

HONORING THE MARRIAGE COVENANT

A covenant is a solemn agreement by both parties, usually sealed by a ritual and having an accompanying sign. For example, after the flood, God promised there would never again be a universal flood. The covenant was sealed by a sacrifice, and then God gave the sign of the rainbow (see Gen. 9:8–16). He also made a covenant with Abraham that had an accompanying sign (see Gen. 15:8–21; 17:10). Perhaps the best example of a covenant is God's agreement with the Israelites at Mount Sinai. Israel agreed to keep God's laws, and God agreed to bless and protect them.

Marriage is a covenant, an agreement between one man and one woman made before God in which they pledge exclusive devotion to each other for life. They seal their covenant by a ritual—the wedding ceremony. The accompanying sign for marriage is not the wedding ring, but sexual intercourse. The Bible says that a man will be "united to his wife, and they become one flesh" (Gen. 2:24). Sex is the culmination of the bonding process between husband and wife and is a continuing force in maintaining the marital bond.

The Importance of Fidelity

Covenants must be honored. The Bible repeatedly shows that God is faithful in keeping his covenants. His faithfulness often contrasts sharply with Israel's unfaithfulness, which the Bible compares to adultery. The life of the prophet Hosea serves as a powerful illustration of the value of faithfulness. God commanded Hosea to marry a promiscuous woman as an illustration of Israel's unfaithfulness to God. When Hosea's wife deserted him, God told him to bring her back, even though she was working as a prostitute (Hos. 1:2; 3:1–2). Hosea's unwavering love for her served as a poignant illustration of God's faithfulness to his covenant obligations. He is faithful, even when we are not. As believers, it's important that we honor our marriage covenants. God intends for us to be faithful to our spouses.

Two of the Ten Commandments reinforce the importance of faithfulness in marriage: the seventh, "You shall not commit adultery," and a portion of the tenth, "You shall not covet your neighbor's wife" (Ex. 20:14, 17). Jesus also strongly affirmed the sanctity of marriage when he cited the Genesis model for marriage, and said, "Therefore what God has joined together, let no one separate" (Matt. 19:6). In fact, Jesus wanted to protect marriage so strongly that he declared the sin of lust to be equivalent to adultery (Matt. 5:28). This elevation of marriage reached a new level when Paul explained that the relationship of a husband and a wife is a model of the spiritual relationship between Christ and his church (see Eph. 5:21, 25–26, 32).

Threats to Fidelity

God wants us to honor our marriage covenants. Yet unfaithfulness is all too common. Many factors threaten marriage and undermine our ability to remain faithful. Two are discussed here.

Premarital Sex. Scripture clearly prohibits sex before marriage, which the Bible labels "sexual immorality" (1 Cor. 10:8; Gal. 5:19; Eph. 5:3; 1 Thess. 4:3). Yet today, many people limit the definition of *sexual immorality* to include only casual or promiscuous sex or adultery. Many people do not think cohabitation or a "committed relationship" is wrong. But the Bible clearly indicates that all sexual relationships outside marriage are harmful. For example, in the law of Moses, if a man had sex with a "virgin who [was] not pledged to be married," he had to marry her (Deut. 22:28–29).

Christ wants the church, his bride, to be "without stain or wrinkle," to be "holy and blameless" (Eph. 5:27). This description mirrors a good spouse's desire for a partner who has not been united with another. To preserve that purity, sex must be reserved for marriage.

In limiting sex to marriage, God aimed to protect the bond between the partners and provide the greatest sexual happiness of the marital couple. Chastity protects us from guilt, unplanned pregnancy, and sexually transmitted diseases. It provides a strong foundation of trust and a more secure relationship in which to raise children. The capacity for human sexual bonding is weakened by a succession of sexual partners. Our culture's high premium on "so-called social experience is contributing to patterns of promiscuity and its defective bonding,"[1] while God's plan for chastity provides for maximum strength pair bonding.

Cultural Influence. The skewed portrayal of human sexuality by the media is another force that undermines marital fidelity. Sexual innuendo fills primetime television and even sneaks into some cartoons. Movies include increasingly graphic sexual content. Pornography is more readily available today than ever.

Jesus taught that thoughts are the seeds of action. He said, "Out of the heart come evil thoughts—murder, adultery, sexual immorality" (Matt. 15:19). He also made clear that sexual sin can be committed with the mind alone: "I tell you that anyone who looks at a woman lustfully has already committed adultery with her in his heart" (Matt. 5:28).

To remain faithful in marriage, we must carefully consider which words and images we allow to enter our minds through the media. We should restrict our exposure to media content that dulls our sensitivity to the horror of sexual sin or, even worse, tempts us to sin. It is impossible to vicariously enjoy immoral behavior and maintain the highest standard of sexual fidelity.

What poses the greatest threat to your sexual fidelity? What will you do to eliminate that risk?

CREATING AN ATMOSPHERE OF LOVE

Many children's stories conclude with "And they lived happily ever after." Anyone who has been married will tell you this is not easy! After the thrilling experience of the wedding, a married couple must establish a home. Two people must learn to live together in harmony. How can they do that? There are at least five elements of a loving home.

Love

God is love, and a Christian home should reflect God's love. But since our culture uses the word *love* to describe everything from a casual affinity ("I love spaghetti") to sexual intercourse ("I make love to my wife"), it is important to define what love really means.

The apostle John explained, "This is how we know what love is: Jesus Christ laid down his life for us. And we ought to lay down our lives for our brothers and sisters" (1 John 3:16). Paul made that even more specific: "Husbands, love your wives, just as Christ loved the church and gave himself up for her" (Eph. 5:25).

Love is a self-giving affection that puts another person's needs above our own. This kind of love does not ask, "What's in this for me?" Rather, it asks, "What does my loved one need?"

Respect

Respect is a second element of a godly home. The Bible defines the respect married people should give each other when the apostle Paul wrote, "Each one of you also must love his wife as he loves himself, and the wife must respect her husband" (Eph. 5:33). The apostle Peter added, "Husbands, in the same way be considerate as you live with your wives, and treat them with respect" (1 Pet. 3:7).

Many couples disrespect each other through their speech. Name-calling and negative labeling all too easily slip into our communication, especially when we're angry. We must guard against that. Public putdowns, even in jest, and condescending speech are disrespectful too. In the place of such selfish speech, loving couples build up one another with words of appreciation, affirmation, and encouragement (see Eph. 4:29; 1 Thess. 5:11). List some ways you can show respect for your spouse.

Responsibility

In a godly family, partners share responsibility and work together to make the family function. That was true in the garden of Eden, and it is true today. The command to "carry each other's burdens" (Gal. 6:2) applies to marriage as well as to other relationships.

Mutual Submission

North American culture teaches the value of independence. That fits well with our natural desire to want things our own way. In a marriage, however, that attitude may lead two people to live separate lives in the same house.

In stark contrast to the prevailing "me first" attitude of our day, the Bible commands couples to "submit to one another out of reverence for Christ" (Eph. 5:21). Often the word *submit* brings to mind the image of authority. That's not what the Bible teaches. In fact, both of the Scriptures that refer to this subject speak to both husbands and wives (see Eph. 5:21–33; 1 Pet. 3:1–12). Submitting to our partners means considering their needs above our own. While the Bible assigns leadership at home to the husband, the concept of mutual submission demands that he be a sacrificial servant leader, as Christ was (see Eph. 5:25).

Permanence

God planned for marriage to be a lifelong union. While Scripture recognizes that divorce is sometimes permissible because of our sin, divorce is not part of God's original plan (see Mal. 2:10, 16; Matt. 19:3–12). The permanence of Christian marriages reflects God's unchangeable love for his people. Divorce, on the other hand, breaks the vow to love "till death do us part."

Like all of God's commands, the command that marriage must be permanent is intended to protect and provide for us. The stability of the marriage is the rock upon which the whole family's emotional stability rests. Everyone thrives in a home that has an atmosphere of permanence.

RAISING GODLY CHILDREN

When God sent his Son into this world as a baby, he chose a human family to instruct, nurture, and be a model for Jesus (Luke 2:51–52). That reinforces the biblical teaching that God ordained the family as the institution to provide for and train children. That shaping process takes place in a number of ways.

Loving

A parent's love teaches children about God's love. We learn about his unconditional love when our parents love us in spite of our childlike shortcomings (see 1 Cor. 13:4–7). We first understand that love is self-sacrificing when we see Mom and Dad putting our needs ahead of their own. From infancy, we learn that love speaks gently as we hear the affectionate words of our parents. A loving home produces loving children.

Actions as well as words must demonstrate love. Five specific actions cause children (and all people) to feel loved: physical touch, quality time, gifts, acts of service, and words of affirmation.[2] Jesus spoke all five love languages in his ministry to people. As our lives show love in all five concrete ways, our homes become sanctuaries of love.

Training

In order to train their children, parents must establish parental authority. Love is the foundation for that authority. Discipline succeeds only when a child knows that he or she is loved.

The Bible says, "Fools despise wisdom and instruction" (Prov. 1:7). Children must be taught the meaning of the word *no* from a young age. The Bible says that parents who truly love their children are "careful to discipline them" (Prov. 13:24). When children grow up in a home with effective discipline, they learn to discipline themselves.

When the foundation of love and authority has been laid, effective training is possible. Scripture admonishes parents to raise their children "in the training and instruction of the Lord" (Eph. 6:4). That task encompasses all of our daily lives. God said, "These commandments that I give you today are to be upon your hearts. Impress them on your children. Talk about them when you sit at home and when you walk along the road, when you lie down and when you get up" (Deut. 6:6–7). Teachable moments can happen in the kitchen, while riding in the car, or while doing daily chores.

Training children also includes instruction in the faith. Loving parents teach their children Bible truth and take them to church, Sunday school, and other healthy learning environments.

Modeling Relationships

Children copy what they see. They first learn how to interact with other people by watching Mom and Dad. This is why it's important for parents to model good relationships, attitudes, and behaviors in their homes. Children remember the parenting and marriage skills they see in their parents and will use them later in life. As we model godly traits such as respectful speech, self-control, appropriately expressing our needs, and controlling our anger, we lay the foundation for our children's future success in their relationships.

Children discover the importance of our beliefs by closely watching the way we live. If we say that worship is important but seldom attend church, our children will learn that worship is of little value.

Children will learn to pray as parents pray with them at bedtime, mealtime, and family devotional times. They need to take part in daily family worship beginning at a young age (see Prov. 22:6). If children see their parents reading the Bible and praying often, they will learn to have their own time alone with God. Talking and praying together about decisions helps children apply Christian values to their own situations. For example, praying as a family about a major purchase teaches children to depend on God for guidance.

Paul's advice to Timothy applies well to parents: "Set an example for the believers in speech, in conduct, in love, in faith and in purity" (1 Tim. 4:12).

What daily situations in your life can serve as opportunities to explain your faith to a child?

NONTRADITIONAL FAMILIES

While the "traditional" family may be ideal, many people find themselves living in other family configurations.

Single Parents

Some parents find themselves alone, raising children without a spouse's aid. Because it is hardly possible to be both mother and father, single parents have a much greater need for support from outside the home.

While the Bible doesn't specifically mention single parenting, it does give instructions about widows and orphans. A single parent is like a widow in that he or she has no partner to encourage and help with the many responsibilities of raising children. Children in single-parent homes miss the benefit of having both a mother and father in the home.

Believers are continually asked to look after widows and orphans (see Isa. 1:16–17; James 1:27). We're also told to carry each other's burdens (see Gal. 6:2). Surely, that means that we should assist single parents when needed. That might include providing babysitting, home or car repairs or financial assistance, or simply spending time with and listening to single parents can show them they are loved and valued.

Singles

Many people in our society are single; some never married, others are divorced, and some are widowed. While God created marriage for our benefit, the Bible also makes it clear that a single lifestyle is an acceptable—even desirable—option for some people (see 1 Cor. 7:1–17). Jesus, after all, was a single adult!

Single adults and those without children can play a significant role in the family life of others by assisting single parents or serving as role models or mentors for young adults. The apostle Paul was like an adopted father to Timothy. Paul's love and encouragement were no doubt instrumental in Timothy becoming a pastor. It is not necessary to have children in order to be a godly influence on younger people.

List some ways you might help a single parent or young person you know.

PROTECTING THE FAMILY

Families face many pressures today. Traditions that were once held dear are now challenged on every side. Families must be intentional about creating and protecting healthy homes. Several areas call for special attention.

The Priority of Marriage

After our relationship with God, marriage is the most important relationship we have. It must come before parental responsibilities, household chores, and jobs. A couple needs time each day to be alone, discuss the events of the day, and express affection. Planning a regular "date" is important for married couples, whether it's going to dinner or taking a walk.

Proper Scheduling

Some common practices in our society can be destructive to family. One of them is busyness. Raising children involves juggling many activities, especially when young people begin to cultivate their own interests. Sports, television, friends, or computer time can crowd out family time. Parents must help children limit outside activities in order to allow adequate time for chores, homework, and especially family activities.

When family members are continually too busy to share a meal together, they are really allowing other things to usurp the place of family time. Busyness may appear to be normal, but it greatly hinders building family relationships.

Outside Influences

Our world's values can creep into the home through television, the Internet, movies, music, and friends. Parents need to constantly monitor the family's input through these channels and be prepared to discuss the unhealthy concepts that will inevitably surface. Parents may need to eliminate some television programs, movies, unsupervised Internet time, and other forms of media.

What movie or television show has your family watched recently? What underlying values did it portray?

Controlling Spending

Materialism is a prominent influence in our society. The Bible teaches us to seek God's kingdom above all else (Matt. 6:33) and to trust God to supply all our needs (Phil. 4:19). By contrast, our culture places great emphasis on wealth and self-sufficiency.

Be wary of the materialism trap. Acquiring more things requires more money and usually more time away from home to earn it. It may be better to invest time in nurturing our children than in working to provide them with more things, especially things they don't need. A good alternative to spending money is to find a community service project that the family can do together. That project will build your family through shared experience and model God's love for others. What are some ministry projects you and your family might work on together?

REFLECTING CHRIST

God created us to reflect his image in our relationships. The lasting loyalty of husband and wife mirrors God's faithfulness to us. As we submit to each other in love, we demonstrate Christ's love for the church. A Christian home is built on love, respect, and care for one another. Children learn to model these qualities from parents who make their faith part of daily life. To protect the family unit, we must prioritize our time well and reject distracting influences. The home becomes the model of compassion in the body of Christ, the church.

NOTES

1. Donald M. Joy, *Bonding: Relationships in the Image of God* (Waco, TX: Word Books, 1985), 42.
2. Gary Chapman and Ross Campbell, *The Five Love Languages of Children* (Chicago: Northfield Publishing, 1997).

Building Deeper Faith Series

The Building Deeper Faith series offers five solid, biblical, five-week group studies—excellent for strengthening those established in faith and grounding those new to it. Each study's five chapters are relevantly designed to be read and considered by group members during a week, followed up by discussion when the group gathers. These studies are non-sequential and can be studied in any order and are powerful, spiritually foundational tools for deeper discipleship.

A Foundation of Faith
978-0-89827-284-0
978-0-89827-285-7 (e-book)

A Spirit of Holiness
978-0-89827-964-1
978-0-89827-965-8 (e-book)

A Life of Discipleship
978-0-89827-965-5
978-0-89827-967-2 (e-book)

A Command to Love
978-0-89827-968-9
978-0-89827-969-6 (e-book)

A Call to Serve
978-0-89827-970-2
978-0-89827-971-9 (e-book)

1.800.493.7539   wphstore.com